Armstrong's Sixth

Armstrong's Sixth

The 2004 Tour de France in Photographs

Text and photographs by
James Startt

Cycle Publishing / Van der Plas Publications, San Francisco

Copyright James Startt, 2005, text and photographs
Printed in Hong Kong

Published by:
Cycle Publishing / Van der Plas Publications
1282 7th Avenue
San Francisco, CA 94122, USA
Tel: (415) 665-8214
Fax: (415) 753-8572
E-mail: con.tact@cyclepublishing.com
Web site: http://www.cyclepublishing.com

Distributed or represented to the book trade by:
USA: Midpoint Trade Books, Kansas City, KS
Canada: Accent Technical Publications, Cambridge, ON
Great Britain: Orca Book Services / Chris Lloyd Sales and Marketing Services,
                Poole, Dorset
Australia: Tower Books, Frenchs Forest, NSW

Cover design: Yvo Design, San Francisco, CA, based on the author's photographs

Frontispiece: Everybody gets excited when the Tour passes by, here photographed
                during the stage 18 team time trial

Photo on this page: Cheered on by spectators, Sebastian Lang, of Germany, climbs
                    the Tourmalet on stage 12

Cataloging in Publication Data
Startt, James, 1962—
Armstrong's Sixth: The 2004 Tour de France in Photographs.
120 p. 28.8 cm
1. Bicycle Racing; I. Authorship; II. Title: The 2004 Tour de France in Photographs
ISBN 1-892495-47-3 (hardcover)
Library of Congress Control Number 2005920662

Acknowledgments

As with every book, thank you's are in store for many. First to Samuel Abt, my longtime traveling partner on the Tour, as well as numerous other cycling adventures. Sam, as a cyclist, your words inspired me to ride faster, and now as a journalist, your work still sets the standard. Your continued support, as well as just plain good company, are invaluable.

I am also greatly indebted to three people in the world of fine arts photography: Paul Kohl and Jeffrey Wolin, my two principal teachers, and Agathe Gaillard, of the Agathe Gaillard Gallery in Paris. All of you maintained an open vision of what qualifies as an artist's personal work and supported my interest in cycling as subject matter.

This book would not have been possible without the continued interest and commitment of Rob Van der Plas at Cycle Publishing / Van der Plas Publications, as well as my two principal employers, *Bicycling* magazine in the U.S., and *Top Vélo* in France—in particular Steve Madden, Bill Strickland, David Speranza, Kris Wagner, Stéphane Guitard, and Olivier Haralambon, who have all provided invaluable support. Many of the stories and pictures in this book first graced their pages.

I also consider myself fortunate to work in a sport where the key event is run by Jean-Marie Leblanc and the Tour de France organization. Thank you for your efforts to keep the event one of integrity, despite the many pressures and demands inherent in modern sport.

Very sincere thanks also goes out to my many colleagues on the road as well as my friends: John Wilcockson, Andy Hood, Joe Lindsey, Rob Arnold, Mark Reidy, Lionel Chami, Gilles Comte, Fred Mons, Greg Shapleigh, Rupert Guiness, John Abt, Philippe Aronson, Emmanuelle Cornet, Eric Francheschi, Phillip Heying, Jerome Soret, Michel Birot, Frankie and Betsy Andreu, Phil Toop, Lisa Scott, Patrick Pizzanelli, John D'Agostino, Marzena Watorek, Francesco Adorno, Robert Roscoe, as well as Gary and Chantal Matoso.

And of course I owe no greater debt than that to my own family. First my parents, Jim and Cathy, who always supported my passions, confident that they would lead into a profession, and now my wife Rebekah and my daughter Ella, who are patient with the many hours I am on the road, and always give me good reason to come home.

Dedicated to the memory of Roger Knoebber, 1939–2004,
raconteur, friend

Introduction

Cycling is not always an easy sport to love—and these days it can be even harder. For many of those who have followed the sport as long as I have, there was a very clear divide, that before the Festina Affair in 1998 and that which followed. Since then, fueled each year seemingly by yet another dopping scandal, question marks fog our perception of the sport.

Yet each year, I like thousands of others keep coming back. Why, I sometimes ask? Apprehension arises as I prepare to leave for each Tour. Nearly four weeks on the road. Four weeks away from home. Four weeks of endless traffic jams. Four weeks fighting for parking. Four weeks fighting for interviews, for pictures. Four weeks of late dinners. Four weeks of bad coffee.

Or worse, will there be another scandal?

But for whatever reason I keep coming back. And after 15 years, I can't imagine life without the Tour. My memory, I now realize, is largely shaped by the Tour. For me, what happened in 1989, in 1996, in 2001 generally starts with who won the Tour that year.

The Tour, however, is much more than the race for the yellow jersey, it is the eternal story of human drama, of human perseverance. In fact, while I have ultimate respect for the race's great champions, I am often even more drawn to the smaller stories, that of the many lesser riders, often faceless riders, who simply strive for a moment of glory or simply to finish. As an amateur cyclist in the 1980's and 90's my own experience was often more akin to theirs. And I never forgot it.

The words and especially the pictures found in this book, therefore, are as much about the participants of this year's Tour as it is about it's winners. Lance Armstrong made history by becoming the first cyclist to win six Tours, a real record in an era where adjectives such as "unprecedented" are increasingly rare. He has dominated his generation like only the greatest before him. But his story needs perspective and it is the many non-winners, the losers and the also rans that give it such a perspective.

The Tour you see would be nothing if it lost its human perspective. The Tour organizers understand this. Each year, despite the race's continued growth, a handful of small towns and villages continue to host a stage start or finish. It's a concerted effort to maintain contact with the roots of the race. And it's well worth the traffic jams one may encounter.

And intuitively it seems, such perspective is understood by both the cyclists and the fans. Throughout the three-week event riders take time before and after each stage to sign autographs or give a child a cap or water bottle. Fans in return line the roads for hours. They cheer for the yellow jersey of course. But they also wait for the last rider to pass, always giving him their encouragement as well.

The Tour has been called cycling's Mass, for here every cyclist is in front of his congregation. Indeed it's a timeless story. And it's one I never seem to tire of telling.

Table of Contents

Introduction 7

Prologue: Looking for the Tour 9

Stage 1: The Deflating Super Hero. 13

Stage 2: Northern Lights Are Yellow. 21

Stage 3: AG2R on Top of the World 25

Stage 4: A Little Bit Above Expectations 31

Stage 5: Voeckler's Baptism 37

Stage 6: His Day in Yellow 41

Stage 7: Crash and Burn 47

Stage 8: The Cradle of French Cycling. 51

Stage 9: The Big Unknown 55

Stage 10: Tricky Rickie is at it Again 61

Stage 11: Ullrich's Secret Weapon. 67

Stage 12: Lance… But of Course. 73

Stage 13: Courage With a Capital "C" 79

Stage 14: Who is Ivan Basso?. 83

Stage 15: Who's Leading T-Mobile? 89

Stage 16: Who'll Get Podium Honors?. 95

Stage 17: The End for Armstrong? 99

Stage 18: Yellow-Jersey Detour. 105

Stage 19: Hungry for Green 111

Stage 20: Armstrong Alone at the Summit 115

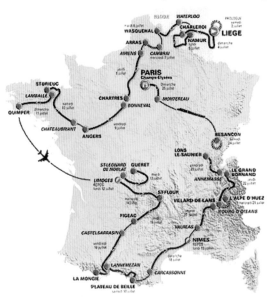

Prologue: Looking for the Tour

THEY'VE tried, the Tour de France organizers, to make the start of this year's race a festive affair. But it's a struggle. Feet, yards, perhaps even miles of white drapes cover the walls of the International Expo Center in Liège, Belgium.

The 2004 Tour started in Liège, Belgium— an unlikely place for a Tour de France perhaps, but then the Belgians love a great bike race as much as the French do.

Still though, the dim fluorescent lights hanging from the steel rafters, reflected a mood that could be described as, well, gloomy at best.

For although everyone wanted to talk about the race ahead—potentially one of the best in years—nobody could avoid the gloom that hung over the sport after a spring full of doping scandals.

First there was the Cofidis Affair, which started slowly with a few of the team's minor members, but in the days prior to the Tour start, the team's top star, David Millar, was placed under formal investigation after admitting taking the banned performance-enhancing drug EPO. Obviously he didn't make the start of this year's Tour. Meanwhile in Spain this spring,

Jesus Manzano, a former rider with the Kelme team, described organized in-depth doping within the team when he raced for them only a year ago. His team is also not welcome at this year's race.

Then in Italy several riders were also placed under investigation, apparently for doping abuses. One of the riders, Danielo DiLuca of the Saeco

team, threatened to start the race. But after showing up in Liège for the start, Tour organizers managed to persuade DiLuca that it was apparently not in his interest to continue. Then on Friday morning, the day before the race started, Gorka Gonzalez of the Euskaltel team failed to pass a blood test and was expelled from the race barely a day before it started.

Above: Swiss rider Fabian Cancellara can hardly believe his eyes. After winning the Prologue, he also became the first rider to wear the yellow jersey in the 2004 Tour de France.

Left: After finishing a close second to little-known Fabian Cancellara, Lance Armstrong can rest easy as his top rivals all finished over 10 seconds behind him, an eternity in a short race like the prologue. In short Armstrong was off to his best Tour start ever.

Then of course, there were the allegations made against five-time defending champion Lance Armstrong in a recent book *LA Confidential*. Written by two award-winning journalists, Irishman David Walsh and Frenchman Pierre Ballester, the book, based on testimony from one-time teammates and team staff members, implies that the American champion himself has used performance-enhancing drugs.

No, life on the road of the Tour de France was not getting off to a good start.

"The ambiance is heavy," said Philippe Brunel, a senior cycling journalist, to the French sports daily *L'Équipe*. "The Tour before was a party. Now it's not too much a party."

"I hear a lot of bad feeling, fear about what's going to happen," said Danish film maker Jorgen Leth, a veteran of 24 Tours and director of the historic cycling film "A Sunday In Hell."

"Many fear police raids like in 1998 [with the Festina and TVM affairs]. People I talk to, who love the sport, the media, are very worried."

And with the riders, there was also a feeling of unease. "Everybody feels the situation is not clear," says Vincent Lavenu, director of the French AG2R team. "Most of the riders feel that real efforts have been made, but that they won't be noticed because of the dopers. They're worried that the guys who have made real efforts are going to be mixed up with those who haven't, and that's not fair."

But somewhere here in Liège, there was talk of an actual bike race. Everyone seems to know that, if the scandals would only subside, this year's Tour could be one of the best in history.

Five-time defending champion Lance Armstrong is going for a legendary sixth Tour victory. But as he said in his press conference this afternoon, "Legend is more than just a six letter word." In terms of his current condition entering the race, he added, "Honestly I don't know where I am. I feel stronger than last year. We'll see."

Armstrong also knew he had more challengers than ever before. "I think this is going to be the hardest Tour

Germany's Jan Ullrich, Lance Armstrong's eternal challenger, joined the pack of the frustrated after the Tour Prologue, finishing in an unimpressive 16th place, a full 15 seconds behind Armstrong. Although the T-Mobile team quickly spun stories that he was sick, Ullrich would soon realize that his Tour preparation had simply not been adequate.

yet. I think we've seen that Jan [Ullrich] is better than he's been, and remains the big rival. After that, there are six or so others, [Iban] Mayo, [Tyler] Hamilton, [Haimar] Zubeldia, [Ivan] Basso that are to make it a tight race."

Hamilton, Armstrong's friend but also rival, said at his own conference, "I think a lot of guys are licking their lips and are ready to attack for sure."

Indeed nearly everybody here for the start of this year's Tour would like to be licking their lips in anticipation. However, the weight of the many doping scandals is making it hard.

American Tyler Hamilton was considered by many to be one of Lance Armstrong's top challengers in the 2004 Tour. However, after finishing the Prologue in 18th position, 18 seconds behind, Hamilton's Tour start was unconvincing and perhaps ominous of the trouble-filled Tour that awaited the amiable Hamilton.

Stage 1: The Deflating Super Hero

ONE MUST wonder just how much more insult sprint legend Mario Cipollini can handle. In his heyday, the rider generally considered the fastest man on two wheels, preferred grandiose nick names like "Super Mario," "Il Magnifico," and the "Lion King." Other stars of lesser egos would certainly have rebuked such monikers. Not the exuberant Cipollini. He has always been sufficiently extroverted to live up to his image.

But lately it's been getting hard. At 37, he is clearly not as fast as he once was. And when it comes to aging athletes, the sport of cycling just has a way of adding insult to injury.

Last year, despite wearing the rainbow-striped jersey as the reigning world champion, he was once again not invited to the race by the organizers of the Tour. Go figure. The man who would be king protested that such a snub was an insult to his world championship title, to his glorious career, not to mention his ego. And he had his fair share of supporters, Tour titan Lance Armstrong among those. Little matter. Race organizers felt giving a boost to the fledgling French team Jean Delatour, sponsored by a strip mall jewelry chain, would better enhance the race.

They cited the fact that Cipollini did not honor the Tour, since he never finished the race. Little matter

A theater of attention always seems to follow the charismatic Mario Cipollini. Despite clearly being at the end of his career, fans still love him, perhaps because he has always loved them and played to them.

that he won an enormous 12 stages when he did compete in the great French race. Many speculated that the Tour organisers simply tired of his dominance, not to mention his taste for extravagant uniforms and occasionally outrageous costumes. After he won four consecutive stages in 1999, the organisers apparently did not approve of his decision to report for stage sign-in dressed as a medieval king. But then, what else should they expect from the man who would be king?

This year, after four years absence, the Tour organizers, in a moment of grace, re-invited the one-time boy wonder. The timing, however, was a little late, as Cipollini has shown virtually no sign of his old spark this year.

After winning two minor races in February, he has consistently taken a back seat to cycling's new speedster, Alessandro Petacchi. Also Italian, Petacchi is virtually Cipollini's alter ego. Where Cipollini is voracious, Petacchi is discreet. In the French sports daily *L'Équipe*, Petacchi said, "the worst criticism someone could give me is that I'm presumptuous." Cipollini, in contrast, defines the word.

At this year's Tour of Italy, Pettacchi consistently outclassed Cipollini in every stage sprint, until Cipollini, humiliated by a crash, decided to abandon.

The Tour de France this year offered him one final chance to redeem himself, not to mention his ego.

Arriving late on the Wednesday night before the Tour at the Eurotel Hotel in Laneken, Belgium, Cipollini appeared tanned but stressed. When one journalist asked him if he could find time for a five-minute interview in the days prior to the Saturday's start

Some of Cipollini's fame rubs off on even his minor teammates on the Domina Vacanze team, as young fans seek autographs from the riders.

of the Tour, he simply glared down and said "no." He did not yet know what he would be doing with his time, but he made it clear that interviews would not be part of it.

Another slightly more fortunate interviewer was given a summary "good," when he queried about the champion's condition.

To fans and autograph seekers he did offer a more positive side. And a wedding party at the hotel was flattered when he agreed to a photo session on Saturday night. But then it was unlikely that either the bride or the groom would pose any disconcerting questions regarding the champion's career or his current condition.

Antonio Ferretti, a Swiss/Italian television journalist and ex-professional said of Cipollini, "Now he's [Cipollini] in a difficult period where he's asking himself questions. I wonder, without cycling, how he'll find a similar ambiance after he stops riding.

It's going to be difficult for him because he loves it so much."

Although Cipollini wasn't talking, his teammates were. But they too were uncertain. "We'll see," said Filippo Simeoni. "He could be good. He could be not good. With Mario you never know. You know he only rode three stages in the Giro and hasn't raced since. He's trained, but hasn't raced."

But this year's Tour is already off to an ominous start for sprinting's one-time master of ceremonies. Only minutes before starting the prologue on Saturday, race officials rebuffed Cipollini's decision to wear a multi-colored full-body skin suit. Citing an arcane ruling against overtly aerodynamic apparel, they forced him to cut off the legs to a level that equaled cyclist's shorts.

With pen in hand, Mario Cipollini prepares to take on the world of autograph seekers prior to the start of stage 1 in Liège, Belgium.

On stage one, a 202-kilometer jaunt from Liège to Charleroi, Cipollini again failed to find his stride. First in the opening kilometers he tangled and tumbled with Spanish climber Oscar Sevilla. And by the end of the day, after struggling over the day's numerous minor climbs, he finished in a forgettable 38th place behind eventual winner Jan Kirsipuu. The race finished in a massive field sprint, normally so well suited to Cipollini. But clearly the sensational sprint star of the past is not the shell of the present.

Things would not improve for Cipollini. After finishing 10th on stage two, he then finished a dismal 95th on stage three. Clearly his days in the Tour were numbered. And after finishing 50th on stage five, the once great and always colorful sprinter had seen enough. Descending into the faceless anonymity of the peloton after 15 years in the limelight was out of the question. He opted not to start stage six. Everyone knew they would never again see Mario Cipollini, likely the greatest sprinter of all time, race the Tour de France again.

"I've obtained everything I can from cycling," he told longtime confidant Philippe Brunel, a journalist for the French sports daily *L'Équipe*, in the opening days of the Tour. "If I wanted to I could close up my suitcases and leave. But I want to understand where I'm at." Clearly he didn't get the answer he came looking for.

Down Is Not Out for Petacchi

He may be Mario Cipollini's alter ego, but in this year's Tour, Alessandro Petacchi, the other Italian sprint star, has mirrored "Super Mario." Both were conspicuously absent from the headlines in the opening week of rac-

Left: Some fans seek to attract more attention than the cyclists.

ing. And sprinters know, if they fail to make their mark on the flat stages so characteristic in the opening week of the great French race, they will have little chance in the two weeks that follow.

The first breakaway in the 2004 Tour de France receives big cheers from a local Belgian boy scout troop.

For the past three seasons, Petacchi has been the world's fastest-rising sprinter. And last year's season was, to date, the crowing achievement for the 31-year-old. In the Tour of Italy he won a superb six stages. In the Tour de France he won another four. And then in September's Tour of Spain he ripped through another five victories for a total of 15, an all-time record in the sport.

This year, he started out even stronger winning an astounding nine stages in the Tour of Italy. Australia's Robbie McEwen was the only other sprinter capable of winning a mass field sprint in the "Giro," as the Italian race is called. And he won only one.

But from the start of this year's Tour de France, despite all expectations, the Italian had clearly lost his stride.

As they do so often, his Fassa Bortolo team accelerated the pace in the final kilometers of the Tour's opening stage, a 202.5-kilometer jaunt through Belgium's Wallone region. In the final kilometers their speed, hovering around 60-kilometers an hour [nearly 40 mph], accelerated unceasingly in an effort to prohibit any other teams from attacking or even positioning their sprinters. But as rarely happens, others followed with relative easy. In the end it was Estonian veteran Jaan Kirsipuu, a plucky second-rate sprinter, but rarely a match for the likes of Petacchi or Cipollini, who won the stage. Petacchi fared no better than eighth.

Facing page: Under the watchful "big eye" monitor screen of the Tour, the pack sprints to the stage 1 finish in Charleroi, Belgium.

Right: Veteran cyclist Jaan Kirsipuu savors his most recent stage victory in the Tour. While not a dominating sprinter, the rider with the French AG2R team always manages to find a way to win a stage in the great French race.

But while a 34-year-old veteran opened the door, a wave of young sprinters would soon dominate this year's race. Twenty-seven-year-old Frenchman Jean-Patrick Nazon would win stage three; 23-year-old Belgian Tom Boonen would win stage six, as well as the final stage into Paris; and 26-year-old Norwegian Thor Hushovd stage eight, after already wearing the yellow jersey for a day.

Meanwhile, Petacchi, like his alter ego Cipollini, slipped into the anonymity of the peloton. He again finished eighth on stage two, before a disastrous 72nd on stage three, and 177th on stage five. He, like Cipollini, failed to start stage six, citing fatigue from the Tour of Italy as well as injuries from a crash.

But Petacchi differed from Cipollini on one point. Although their Tours ended on the same low note, Petacchi at least knew that at the age of 31 he was still in his peak years and there would be more Tours awaiting him.

Italian sprint star Alessandro Petacchi appears introspective after stage 3, where he once again failed to win the sprint finish.

Stage 2: Northern Lights Are Yellow

"I'M NERVOUS," said Norwegian cyclist Thor Hushovd prior to the start of stage two in this year's Tour de France. Why the butterflies you ask? Well, because the amiable Credit Agricole team rider had a real chance to win the famed yellow jersey by the end of the day.

yellow jersey. A muscular rider, he possesses a fine sprint, but he is simply not built for the mountains of the Tour. However, by performing well in

Since the start of the 2004 season Hushovd has created a quiet revolution, winning no less than seven races in France. And for weeks now he's been talking about the Tour de France.

Usually he speaks of the green jersey, generally awarded to the top overall sprinter in the race, not the

Norwegian cyclist Thor Hushovd talks with the press before the start of stage 2 and contemplates the possibility of taking over the yellow jersey at the end of the stage. Hours later such thoughts became reality. Finishing second, he picked up enough bonus seconds to move ahead into the overall lead, a first for Hushovd as well as for Norway.

the Tour prologue on Saturday, he began this year's race only 10 seconds out of the lead. And by winning a bonus sprint Sunday on stage one as well as finishing third he took over the green jersey and moved to within only two seconds of yellow.

His success has also revitalized his French Credit Agricole team, which has a long tradition of developing foreign cyclists. The team's director

Roger Leageay coached American Greg LeMond to his third Tour de France title in 1990, and in recent years has garnered moderate success with Germany's Jens Voigt and Australia's Stuart O'Grady. But when the two left at the end of 2003, many wondered how they would remain in the top tier of professional cycling.

Enter Hushovd

"When Stuey [O'Grady] left the team, I felt I had to do his job and mine. But I like it. And when the team works for

Above: As the Tour de France spent its first three days in Belgium, makeshift memorials to the legendary Eddy Merckx could be seen in many places along the roadside. Here, an old poster in the window shows Merckx advertising chewing gum.

Left: American Lance Armstrong hurries to the sign-in area in Charleroi. Although he is laying low in the opening week of the race, he appears focused on the task at hand—winning yet another Tour.

Facing page: Local Belgian cyclists put down their bikes momentarily to watch stage 2 of the Tour pass by.

me, I want to provide." What Hushovd aspired to do, O'Grady had already accomplished, twice winning the yellow jersey in the Tour by using his turn of speed to nibble away and gain time in the many bonus sprints littered throughout the opening week.

Standing in the shadows of his new star, Hushovd's director Leagay couldn't be more pleased with his star. "In my opinion, he's one of the great riders of the future for stage wins in the Tour, the green jersey or the classics. He's a winner. I signed him when he was 19, and immediately we set out a career plan for him. Already in his first Tour two year's ago, he won a stage. And now at 26, he's just hitting his stride."

Hushovd may well be a man now. But on this morning, he still kept some of his boyish enthusiasm. Winning the yellow jersey would be a dream come true, he said. But he was also realistic. "We'll just have to wait and see," he said. "If I'm in a position, I'll go for the bonus sprints. But the first one isn't until 53-kilometers after the start, so there might be a breakaway. Then I'll just have to concentrate on the final sprint."

Throughout the stage, a 197-kilometer jaunt through Belgium's Wallone region from Charleroi to Namur, Hushovd rode with iron-like resolve. Despite an early breakaway that predictably kept any bonus sprints out of the hands of the sprinters in the pack, Hushovd rode a brilliant field sprint to the line, avoiding a massive crash in the final meters, to finish second, hence garnering an additional 12 bonus seconds, sufficient to take the yellow jersey.

Screaming across the line, many watching thought he was the winner rather than Robbie McEwen of Australia.

Later at the post-race press conference he remained jubilant. "It [winning the yellow jersey] is the biggest thing that can happen in the Tour. Tomorrow I'd like to win the stage in the yellow jersey, but I'd also like to protect the green jersey."

Swiss cyclist Fabian Cancellara prepares for the start of stage 2 in Charleroi, Belgium, and savors yet another day in the yellow jersey. It would be his last.

Stage 3: AG2R on Top of the World

FRENCH TEAM DIRECTOR Vincent Lavenu has been all smiles during these first days of the Tour de France. Those who know the sometimes austere director, however, know that he is not prone to overt optimism.

Frenchman Jean-Patrick Nazon, of the AG2R team, rejoices afer winning stage 3, one of the many early successes for the team.

A small-time pro in the 1980's, Lavenu has directed various and sundry professional teams for nearly 15 years now. Some, like the Casino team back in 1997 and 1998, were real powerhouses. Others, like Chazal, a sausage company, could be described as pack fodder... at best.

Most days, his current AG2R team is unremarkable, not fodder, no, but certainly no world beaters. But thanks to the team's two sprinters, Jaan Kirsipuu and Jean-Patrick Nazon, the team has suddenly dominated this year's Tour in unexpected fashion. Kirsipuu won the Tour's opening stage and Nazon came away victorious the next day on stage three, a

210-kilometer jaunt from Waterloo, Belgium to Wasquehal, France.

Although the 35-year-old Kirsipuu and the 27-year-old Nazon have both won stages in the Tour de France before, they generally take a back seat to speed kings like Mario Cipollini or Alessandro Petacchi.

Cipollini, who has won 12 Tour stages, and Petacchi, who has won five, however, have been uncharac-teristically off-key in this year's Tour. So far, neither has managed to even place in the top five of a stage. Petacchi appears tired after winning no less than nine stages recently in the Tour of Italy, while Cipollini simply seems tired. Fifteen years as a top professional, it seems, will wear down even cycling's greatest stars.

Meanwhile AG2R is having a veritable ball during the early stages of this year's Tour.

Above: Spanish cyclist Roberto Heras makes his way to the sign-in for stage 3 amidst the carnavalesque spirit of the Tour.

Left: Tattered, torn and bloodied, Spanish climber Iban Mayo, the Tour's first principal victim, fields questions from the Spanish press. Crashing before the race crossed the cobblestones of the legendary Paris–Roubaix race, the Spanish climber finished nearly four minutes down on the main field. It proved to be the first difficult day of what would soon be a disastrous race for the promising rider.

Facing page: Wearing the yellow jersey, Thor Hushovd races past Belgian fans on the cobbles. His tenure in the yellow jersey would be short-lived, as he finished well off the pace.

"You know it's not always easy having two sprinters on the same team," Lavenu said. "But so far it's working well. The important thing is to be stronger with two, not weaker." Prior to the start of the Tour, Lavenu was uncertain how to define the team strategy. "The two are very different. Jaan is cold-blooded and never pan-

ics. J.P. is more of a thoroughbred. Everything needs to be in place for him. Finally, Lavenu said, the two riders work it out among themselves. "They communicate in the final kilometers."

Next to Lavenu, Nazon was relaxed, but focused on the stage that held much promise for him. "We're just starting. We're feeling each other out. We try not to build the team

uniquely around any one rider. The guys aren't real lead-out specialists. It's not like with Petacchi's team or Cipollini's team. All those guys are paid to lead their sprinter out just perfectly. Not here, so you can't expect them to get a real train rolling, but they help us out when they can."

Unlike 34-year-old Kirsipuu, who thrives on his hard-work ethic that has won him over 100 races, Nazon spent

most of his first years as a professional overweight and in obscurity. But he suddenly blossomed last year after nearly finding himself out of a job. Riding then for the Jean Delatour team, he responded by winning the final stage in last year's Tour as well as wearing the yellow jersey earlier in the race. This year, he is clearly more confident. "I've still got the same legs," he laughed. "but in my head it's better."

"I hope to win soon," he said after finishing fifth on the first stage and third on stage two.

Soon, in fact, came four hours 36 minutes and 45 seconds after the start of stage three. Braving two cobblestone roads featured in the Paris–Roubaix race that split the peloton in

Left: The shadow from an unidentified rider rolls toward the start of stage 3 in Waterloo, Belgium.

Facing page: Frenchman Jean-Patrick Nazon (second from left) scored the second stage win in three days for the modest AG2R team. Veteran German sprinter Erik Zabel (left) could only look on in frustration.

half, Nazon and Kirsipuu both stayed near the front until Nazon powered away on the uphill finish.

"Jaan came up to me in the final kilometers and told me he thought it wasn't his day and he would help me. In the past I've always been on teams where sprinters were always playing their own card. But here, to have an older guy like Jaan come up and ride for you. Well that just gives you confidence."

In a long list of celebrities that follow the Tour, singer and guitar slinger Ben Harper made his Tour debut in Waterloo, Belgium.

Stage 4: A Little Bit Above Expectations

DOUBT AND SPECULATION surrounded the U.S. Postal team prior to the start of this year's Tour de France, as the competition finally appeared to be catching up to five-time defending champion Lance Armstrong.

But already there are very clear signs that Armstrong and his U.S. Postal team are as strong as ever, and the competition, while improving, still must contend with a hungry champion.

First there was the 6.1-kilometer prologue in Liège, Belgium. Many thought it was ideal for a rider like Jan Ullrich, Armstrong's longtime rival, since it was filled with long straight roads and only a few tricky turns. But the German failed, never really hitting his stride, while Armstrong unleashed his best prologue performance ever.

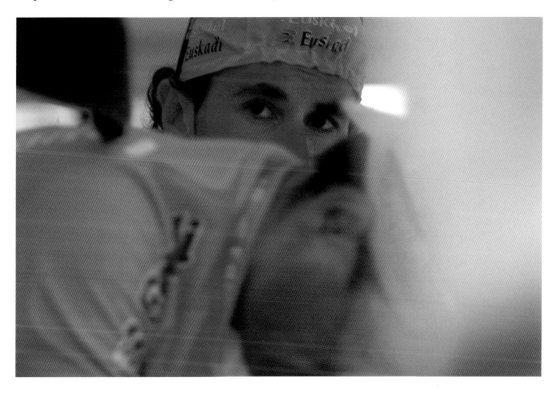

Spaniard Iban Mayo appears reflective before the start of the team time trial, after crashing and losing nearly four minutes on stage 3 the day before.

31

Although he narrowly missed stage victory to Italian Fabian Cancellara, he left Ullrich 17 seconds behind, nearly three times as much as he had gained on his German rival in any year past. Much improved Tyler Hamilton, after Armstrong the top American in the 2004 Tour, was 18 seconds behind, while up-and-coming

Spaniard Iban Mayo was 21 seconds behind, and Roberto Heras, another Spaniard and top climber 37 seconds behind.

Equally impressive was the Postal's overall performance in the prologue, placing four riders in the top 20.

"It was good for all of us," said American Floyd Landis. "We all wanted to see what would happen with Ullrich and the other favorites, and I think we were all pleasantly surprised. It's a good start."

The next crucial moment came when the Tour crossed over two cobble-stone roads known from the infamous Paris–Roubaix race on stage three. It was the first time in nearly 20 years that the Tour rode over cobbles, and many feared that top Tour riders could be severely penalized with crashes or flats.

Team director Johan Bruyneel spoke for many when he said, "For sure today you cannot win the Tour de France, but you can lose the Tour de France."

Armstrong, who has never ridden Paris–Roubaix was apprehensive, but he couldn't have had a better team, as riders like George Hincapie and Viatcheslav Ekimov are considered two of the world's best cyclists over cobbles.

Despite the fierce fighting for position in the kilometers prior to the first cobbles, Armstrong rolled through them in third place, tucked neatly behind Hincapie and Ekimov. Spanish rival Iban Mayo, who has no experience on the cobbles and has no teammates with any significant experience, faired much worse. Crashing just be-

Facing page: A member of the local cycling club looks on in admiration as the Spanish Euskaltel team passes at the start of the stage 4 team time trial.

Right: The Italian Saeco team pounds through the town of Marcoing during the team time trial.

fore the first section, he eventually finished 3 minutes 56 seconds down.

Suddenly Armstrong had one less contender for the yellow jersey.

And the team time trial the following day provided yet another occa-

Facing page: Lance Armstrong's U.S. Postal team rounds the last corner and heads for the finish line of the team time trial in Arras. After one of the best team performances ever, Armstrong suddenly found himself in the yellow jersey early in the race. Although pleased to be well placed among his rivals, Armstrong nevertheless would not defend the jersey so early into the race.

Below: A lone cyclist weathers the storms to encourage the Brioches les Boulangère team during the wet and windy stage 4 team time trial.

sion for Armstrong and his team to continue their roll.

While they received stiff competition from Hamilton's Phonak squad and Ullrich's T-Mobile team, the Postmen gave everyone a lesson in how to best ride this very technical event, winning it for the second straight year.

Clearly they were the best organized and most experienced team in this discipline. While Hamilton and Ullrich are both riding with new teams, Armstrong has ridden with many of his teammates in years past. Such experience and familiarity pays off in a team time trial.

"The team this year was even better [than last year]," Armstrong said afterward. "We started slow, but when we started going it was really unbelievable. I was just smiling on the bike. It was like a dream."

The victory also thrust Armstrong into the yellow jersey as the overall individual rider in the race. It is a position Armstrong knows well, as he has already worn the coveted shirt for nearly 60 days in his career. "That's two months of my life," he calculated quickly in the evening post-stage press conference. But he also hinted strongly that he would not yet defend the jersey, as it was too early in this year's Tour, and he didn't want to waste the energy of his teammates before the race hit the mountains later in the race.

Undoubtably, Armstrong had his best Tour debut ever, and he appeared genuinely relaxed despite the daunting challenge that lies before him—that of becoming the first rider in history to win the Tour de France.

"I would say our Tour performance is a little bit above our expectations," director Johan Bruyneel said after the team time trial victory. "Overall it's been great."

Indeed few would argue.

The U.S. Postal team was all smiles after winning the stage 4 team time trial.

Stage 5: Voeckler's Baptism

T HE TOUR DE FRANCE got religion today as stage five of this year's race started and finished in two towns—Amiens and Chartres—famous for their magnificent Gothic Cathedrals. But for Tour de France cyclists, their cross is the yellow jersey.

And today, after weathering stiff winds and pounding rains, 24-year-old French professional Thomas Voeckler survived a 184-kilometer breakaway to take over the coveted golden fleece in an impressive manner.

When it rains, it pours. Or so it is said. But while most of the 180-odd Tour cyclists were brooding about the weather, Voekler was basking in a string of successes that shows no signs of letting up. Only 10 days before the start of this year's Tour, Voeckler became the French national champion. And now he must trade in the distinctive blue, white and red jersey worn

Moments after the finish, French national champion Thomas Voeckler is only just beginning to realize that his life would forever change. As the best-placed rider in the winning breakaway, Voeckler took a nearly 10-minute lead on the Tour's top competitors. It was a lead he would hold for half of the race, a feat that would forever etch his name in the hearts and minds of Tour fans.

by the national champion for the coveted yellow jersey donned by the race leader of the Tour.

It's a change Voeckler nevertheless is willing to make. "The last days have been crazy," he said. "So much attention. So many interviews. I can't lie. I can't say nothing has changed. But I think I'm still not realizing it."

Voeckler's path toward cycling's summit, however, has been an untra-ditional one. Growing up in the French Carribean island of Marti-nique, he led a Huckleberry Finn ado-lescence, filled with hours of fishing and boating. But those days ended abruptly when his father disappeared, lost at sea.

Solace soon came through cy-cling. By the time he was in his late teens, his mother sent him to high school in France, and soon he signed with the Vendée U amateur cycling team, the farm club for the Brioches le Boulangère professional team.

Known for his feisty, aggressive approach to racing, Voeckler soon made name for himself as a fearless breakaway rider, and this year this at-titude is paying off.

Entering today's stage in the Tour, Voeckler knew he had his card to play. After winning the yellow jersey

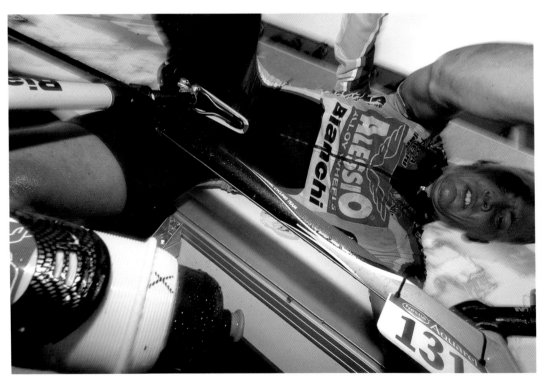

Above: Italian Mario Cipollini appears strangely jovial after a miserable day in the rain. Does he already know that this would be his last day in the Tour de France?

Left: Swedish rider Magnus Backstedt is exhausted and visibly frustrated to finish no better than fifth, after spending nearly all of stage 5 in the breakaway.

in the team time trial yesterday, five-time Tour champion Lance Armstrong announced that it was too early in the race for him and his U.S. Postal teammates to begin defending the lead. "We [Voeckler and his teammates] all knew that it was worth trying to get into a breakaway."

But, like in the national championships, it was Voeckler, and not his teammates who made the decisive move.

Jumping free with four others—Australia's Stuart O'Grady, Sweden's Magnus Backstedt, Denmark's Jakob Piil, and fellow Frenchman Sandy Casar— only 16 kilometers into the stage, Voeckler, the best placed rider in the bunch, suddenly found himself the yellow jersey on the road, as the group forged an impressive 16-minute lead.

Armstrong, as promised, put up little fight. And while O'Grady won the

stage, Voeckler, who finished fourth, won the jersey with a 3 minute 13 second lead over O'Grady in second place and 9 minute 35 second lead over Armstrong, the race's top contender.

But while Voeckler made it clear that he hoped to defend the jersey, he had no illusions of still having it when the race finally returns to Paris. "I'm not going to play in their game," he said referring to the expected fight for the yellow jersey between Armstrong and rivals—his countryman Tyler Hamilton or Jan Ullrich of Germany. "I'm just not at the same level. I'm not thinking about the overall. The Tour is really a level above all other races in the year. I'll give my maximum. I'll keep it as long as possible, but…"

Right: Lance Armstrong appears relieved to have finished the long, wet stage from Amiens to Chartres. Little matter that he lost the yellow jersey, the crucial battles of the race were still days away.

Stage 6: His Day in Yellow

WHILE THE TOUR rolled through the endless wheat fields that constitute France's own heartland, a 196-kilometer stage fit for a yawn, 24-year-old Thomas Voeckler spent his first day in the yellow jersey.

And although Lance Armstrong has spent a mammoth 60 days of his career wearing this same shirt, for most professionals, even one day is a dream.

Just ask Thor Hushovd, who wore the coveted yellow jersey on stage three. "For me it was one of the biggest days of my career—no it was the biggest. I think it changed something. I'm getting more popular."

Jean-Patrick Nazon, the sprinter with the AG2R team, held the same honor just a year ago. "It's hanging in a frame in my house. What a moment of emotion! Unforgettable."

"I was surprised by the effect of the yellow jersey," said Voekler at the finish. "Everyone was patting me on the back. And people clapped for me from the first to the last kilometer. Really special."

For many a cyclist, a day in yellow is the defining moment of their career. For some, it can erase an otherwise

Facing page: Frenchman Thomas Voeckler leads the pack through the wheat fields of France's heartland at the start of stage 6, his first day in the yellow jersey.

Right: Spanish climber Oscar Sevilla was just one of the many victims on the crash-filled final into Angers. His teammate Tyler Hamilton also saw his Tour chances severely compromised in the same crash.

forgettable career. But for others, it can also transform them, giving them newfound confidence.

Voeckler, according to just about everyone here at the Tour de France, is likely to be of the later category and many expected him to hold onto the jersey for days to come. After all, he had an enviable 9 minute and 35 second advantage over Tour favorite Lance Armstrong.

"He can hold it to the Pyrenees or even longer," said French champion

Right: Frenchman Thomas Voeckler signs autographs during his first day in the yellow jersey on stage 6.

Below: Always the center of attention, German star Jan Ullrich talks with reporters after stage 6. He was one of the few to avoid the many crashes.

Laurent Jalabert, who twice wore the yellow jersey briefly.

Although this was the first day that Voeckler, as well as all his Brioches Le Boulangère teammates, have ever defended the lead in a race like the Tour de France, they appeared to take lessons from the US Postal team when it came to composure.

Like Armstrong, Voeckler crashed in a mass pile-up only 13 kilometers into the race, but he quickly got up and resumed chase. Less than 10 kilometers later, a six-rider breakaway scampered away, but Voeckler's team never let the group get more than a four and half-minute gap. Not sufficient against the steady headwinds that continued through the day.

"At the team meeting this morning, we said that we could let a group get away, but no more than six riders."

Nevertheless, Voeckler said the day was stressful. It was for others as

Above: Belgium's Peter Farazijn, a last-minute replacement on the Codifis team, survived the many crashes to finish stage 6.

Left: After winning Stage 6 into Angers, Belgian Tom Boonen confirmed why he is considered one of the most promising sprinters for years to come.

well, as another mass crash in the final kilometer splintered the field at the finish. Nevertheless he easily held onto the overall race lead at the finish, hence qualifying to wear the jersey for yet another day, if not more.

Already predictions abound concerning just how long the previously unknown Frenchman can hold onto his lead. "Until La Mongie," according to Armstrong, who felt that the 24-year-old would crack on the first day in the Pyrenees. Others, however, noted that Voeckler is a sturdy climber, who recently won the Route du Sud, a three-day event also held in the Pyrenees. For them, Voeckler could easily carry the shirt into the Alpes and into the final week of the Tour de France— perhaps even longer.

But then the Tour de France is nothing if not three weeks of perpetual speculation.

Above: Crash and burn in the Tour de France. Stage 3 winner Jean-Patrick Nazon nurses his wounds after a crash erased his chances on stage 6.

Left: At the finish of stage 6, Frenchman Thomas Voeckler savors his first full day in the yellow jersey.

Stage 7: Crash and Burn

WHY SO MANY crashes this year? Actually, stage 7 was an uncharacteristic day in the Tour: It was a day with no major crashes, no heavy casualties. With the first week of this year's Tour now over, the race so far can be described as an eventful one—but also a dangerous one.

In a rare bit of down time, Jan Ullrich stops to sign autographs with local children prior to the start of stage 7 in Chateaubriand in France's western province of Brittany.

"Before, when we neared the finish, we thought about winning. Now we just think about falling," Jean-Patrick Nazon told the French sports daily *L'Équipe* this morning. Nazon, who rides for the AG2R team and won stage three, crashed yesterday in the mass pile-up with just one kilometer to go.

All but about 20 riders made it past that crash, the second major accident of the day. Of the major candidates for the yellow jersey, only Jan Ullrich has yet to kiss the concrete. Lance Armstrong, Tyler Hamilton, and Iban Mayo have all been slowed by crashes. Mayo, however, is the only one to have lost significant time, when a crash cost him nearly four minutes on the stage to Wasquehal.

"I'm sore," said American Bobby Julich, who went down in the same crash at the end of stage 6. "Everyone is trying to use the same tactic as the U.S. Postal team—to have everyone stay around the leader at the front. Phonak is doing it, T-Mobile is doing it, Euskaltel is doing it. We're doing it. And nobody wants to give."

In addition, with top sprinters like Mario Cipollini or Alessandro Petacchi no longer in the race after failing to start stage six, the big sprint teams, those most capable of keeping the pace high in the final kilometres, are no longer present. As a result, there is an intense fight for positioning in the last kilometers.

But everyone seems to agree that the weather conditions have also heightened the element of danger.

"It's the wind," said Australian rider Stuart O'Grady, who won stage 5 and took over the green points jersey. "Definitely the wind is causing havoc, so much carnage. If there wasn't the wind, there would be no problem."

"The whole first week has been just really, really nervous. Everybody wants to be in the front There's just not enough spaces for everyone. So there are crashes," Swiss rider Sven Montgomery said, when speaking about crashing in his team hotel before the start of stage 5.

Montgomery knows a thing or two about crashing, for while he has started six major three-week Tours, he

Left: French veteran Laurent Brochard rolls toward the showers after finishing fourth on stage 7.

Facing page: Fans applaud as the Tour passes through a village in Brittany.

Facing page: Scott Sunderland (right), Paolo Bettini (center), and Stuart O'Grady (left) lead the pack across line at the finish of stage 7.

Below: FDJ.com rider Carlos DaCruz enjoys a visit from his daughter in the team car prior to the start of stage 7.

has never managed to finish one. In 2001, he crashed heavily while descending in the final week of the Tour, cracking his skull. And barely a month before the start of this year's Tour de France, he crashed out of the Tour of Italy, breaking his right shoulder.

"I'm kind of scared because of all the crashes I've had," he continued. "For now I can't do anything else. So I'm always riding at the back. I can't take any risks. My personal goal is just to see Paris."

But even in the back, it's not always easy to avoid danger. Montgomery, among others crashed on stage five into Chartres, and finished well behind the pack.

For most riders, today's stage, with more sun, and less rain, was a pleasant one. Not for Montgomery, however, who was one of the day's principal victims. Crashing again, this time 127 kilometers into the stage, he broke his right collar bone.

His hope to finally finish the Tour, to finally see Paris, once again came to an end.

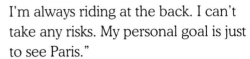

After winning stage 5, Australian rider Stuart O'Grady took control of the green points jersey awarded to the most consistent sprinter in the race. His tenure would be short-lived this year.

Stage 8: The Cradle of French Cycling

"**I**N BRITTANY this is sunshine," said a local at the Tour de France start today, after heavy showers turned to drizzle. The northwestern French region of Brittany, and the local Bretons, are a strange breed indeed, but they also make pretty good cyclists.

Bernard Hinault, Lucien Petit-Breton, Jean Robic, Louison Bobet, Cyril Guimard, the list is long. Brittany's own constitute a large part of French cycling history. And that history was celebrated today as the Tour crossed through the cradle of French cycling in a 168-kilometer stage from the northern village of Lamballe to the southern town of Quimper.

The current wave of Breton cyclists—Frederic Guesdon, Sebastian Hinault, Ludovic Martin, Jean-Cyril Robin—have been less illustrious than their predecessors, but career highlights mattered little today. All Breton cyclists were heroes.

A concentrated Tyler Hamilton makes his daily trip toward stage sign in prior to the start of stage 8.

As the race rolled through another rain-drenched day, some wondered if this year's Tour would ever see real sunshine, and not the disputable version known in Brittany?

Prior to the start of this year's Tour, many were predicting another heat wave similar to the one that dominated last year's race. "It's going to be hot again," said retired French champion Laurent Jalabert. When asked to reveal his source, he simply shrugged and said, "I know, the peasants told me."

Among his many post-cycling activities, Jalabert oversees his own vineyards. In theory, such work should keep him in tune to the pulse of the land. Yet even to a seasoned vintner, mother nature, knows how to hide her cards.

At this year's Tour, Jalabert works as a commentator for French television. When he was reminded of his

Above: Fans of all ages weather the rains to watch the start of stage 8 in Lamballe.

Right: Prior to every stage start, riders stop to stock up on a variety of sport nutrition foods and drinks.

pre-Tour prediction while scampering toward his car under a protective umbrella, he simply laughed, "Oh those peasants. "*C'est incroyable*," it's incredible. What do they know?"

Regardless, the day was filled with huge crowds fit for an otherwise sunny day. But then rain here, is sun, right?

"Cycling has been part of our culture from way back," said Bernard Hinault, a five-time Tour de France winner and Brittany's number-one son. "Every village has races, plus the climate here, the wind, the rain, forge strong cyclists. Those who succeed in cycling here are really strong in the head."

Bretons are also known for their independent spirit, as their Gaellic roots transcend French borders and nationality. In that regard they are not different from the Basque people in the south. Fiercely independent, they

Above: For some, like Spain's Angel Vicioso Arcos, the Tour de France promises to be one long, strange trip.

Right: Fig. 8.5. French rider Frederic Guesdon, one of the local heros from Brittany, enjoys a visit with his family in the start village prior to hitting his region's roads.

For Irish cyclist Mark Scanlon, World Junior Champion in 1998, his debut in the 2004 Tour was a learning experience.

are as likely to wave the black and white Breton flag as they are the blue, white and red flag of France. They are a people who work the land as well as the surrounding seas. They are a simple people, little interested in luxury and ease.

"It's the sport of the region," says Frederic Guesdon, currently ranked 86th in this year's race. "The terrain is great, very mixed, with lots of minor roads perfect to ride on. And then there is the history, the champions, Bobet, Hinault. That's what got me into it."

Only too often, though, a Tour visit to Brittany lends itself to unflattering comparisons of champions of the past to those of the present. Hinault was the last Frenchman to win the Tour back in 1985. Riders like Guesdon, though capable of winning the grueling Paris–Roubaix classic back in 1997, can hope for no more than a stage win in a race like the Tour.

But today, a week into the 2004 Tour de France, the comparisons are less embarrassing. The French can thank the little-known Thomas Voeckler for that. He captured the yellow jersey after a long breakaway on stage five into Chartres and has nearly a ten-minute lead on race favorites like Lance Armstrong, Tyler Hamilton, and Jan Ullrich.

It's a lead that is not likely to last until Paris. But today at least, as well as on Bastille Day, the French national holiday, now only days away, Voeckler's yellow jersey promises to keep the French in a festive mood.

Stage 9: The Big Unknown

THE TOUR DE FRANCE will soon take another turn as it begins the first of several climbing stages. Nine climbs await the Tour riders as they cover a grueling 240 kilometers in the Massif Central region.

Speculation abounds concerning the favorites for the yellow jersey. Lance Armstrong of course is on everyone's lips, but so are Tyler Hamilton and Jan Ullrich. Surprisingly, another name is garnering attention—that of American veteran Bobby Julich.

Once, some still remember, America's great hope in stage racing was not Armstrong but Julich, now 32. And after finishing third in the 1998 Tour de France, Julich was in prime position to win the world's greatest bike race himself . But that was before a crash dashed his 1999 Tour chances. And it was before Armstrong took definitive control of the great French race. With the rise of

Armstrong, Julich faded into obscurity. Lacking results, he finally became a simple team rider—an unlikely end for a talent like Julich.

This year, however, Julich rediscovered his winning condition, and suddenly he appears to be a factor in this year's Tour.

"I wish I could have bottled up that feeling and kept it," says Julich of the condition that carried him up the steps of the Tour podium in 1998. "That was a magic year, out of the

Frenchman Giles Bouvard, reading the morning paper in the start village, which is just one of many morning traditions in the Tour.

blue, where everything went well. Then it just fell apart. And once that snowball starts rolling downhill, it's hard to stop."

Problems started midway through the Metz time trial in the 1999 Tour. Hearing that he was over a minute behind the favorites, Julich, who was then the leader of the French Cofidis team, started taking chances, trying desperately to cut his losses.

Instead, he ended up in the ditch in a long off-camber turn. His tour was over.

A year later, he moved to the French Credit Agricole team in an effort to reignite his career. Instead, he met with more mediocre results. Finally, he moved to the German Telekom team. By now, he was no longer a team leader, but rather a support rider to stars like Jan Ullrich, Alexander Vinokourov, and Erik

Zabel. It was a job he fullfilled well enough. He's a good soldier, and he shouldered the responsibility honorably. But somehow his position didn't seem fitting.

Discouraged at the end of the 2003 season, Julich was on the verge of returning to race in the United States before finally retiring. But that was before he received an offer to

1996 Tour winner Bjarne Riis to ride for his Danish CSC team.

Riis, along with the CSC organization, it seems, have finally been able to uncork Julich's real potential once more, so often buried under his own insecurities and pressures, so often beaten by his own demons.

Like Julich, Riis is known for his meticulous, sometimes scientific approach to training. And he has also

Facing page: Always a party when the Tour passes.

Right: Leading the way, the caravan pulls out of St.-Leonard-de-Noblat before the start of stage 9.

earned the reputation as a director that fosters team spirit. "I'm much more respected in this team than in previous teams. Yeh, I feel like I know my place. Bjarne makes us feel like we're all leaders. Everyday he comes and asks every rider: How are you? How are you feeling? Are you happy?"

Julich says his training has changed dramatically. Gone are the countless hours of long, steady distance rides. Currently, he includes much more interval training in his program. Working with the SRM training system that is based on watts power output, Julich downloads and sends each day's training data to Riis, so that they can modify and maximize each workout.

Results came quickly this year, as he finished a strong third in the Paris–Nice race in March, behind his teammate and overall winner Jorg Jachshe. And then he won the time trial in Spain's Tour of the Basque Country in April.

"For sure, he's one of the satisfactions of the year," Riis said prior to the start of stage 9 today. "It's a victory for Bobby, a victory for us, a victory for everybody. Clearly, he refound his motivation. I can see he likes the team. He does everything 100%."

As the Tour approaches the mountains, Julich sits in 22nd place. He is looking forward to the climbing. After all, he is only a minute behind Lance Armstrong, currently in 6th place, 9 minutes and 35 seconds on

Left: In the Quick Step team bus, Richard Virenque attaches a portable radio to his teammate Laurent Dufauz before the start of stage 9.

Facing page: Australian Robbie McEwen, wearing the green points jersey, showed that he was one of most consistent sprinters in the 2004 Tour by winning his second sprint on stage 9 into Gueret.

first-place Thomas Voeckler of France, and only 5 seconds behind Germany's Jan Ullrich.

But Julich also knows that he could be an early casualty, that the high mountains of this year's Tour may still be out of his realm. He's realistic, but he's also optimistic.

"I'm not saying I'm on the level with Lance and Ullrich. But I'm not saying I'm not. It feels like 1998 again. It's a big unknown."

Below: Wearing the green points jersey after winning his second victory on stage 9, Robbie McEwen fields questions from the press.

Above: Italian classics specialist Paolo Bettini relaxes in the team bus prior to the start of stage 9 in St.-Leonard-de-Noblat. Following the tactics of his Quick Step team, Bettini raced for the polka-dot jersey awarded to the best climber throughout the first half of the Tour. This move helped his teammate Richard Virenque, effectively keeping the jersey out of the reach of any of Virenque's rivals.

Stage 10: Tricky Rickie is at it Again

SUBTLETY IS NOT a strength when it comes to French climber Richard Virenque. No, just about everyone in this year's Tour de France knew that once the mountains came, the 34-year-old Frenchman would be attacking.

Step team, and the man generally credited with salvaging the French rider's career from his own self-im-

And just about everyone knew that he would do it on this first mountain stage from Limoges to St.-Flour, a riddling 240-kilometer stage with no less than nine moderate climbs.

After all, today was Bastille Day, the French national holiday, and about the only thing Virenque loves more than climbing mountains, is showing off to his fans.

"I've never seen anyone quite like him," said Patrick Lefevere, Virenque's director on the Belgian Quick

With the mountains only a day away, French climber Richard Virenque is in a reflective mood. Soon he will try to become the first climber to win the polka-dot King of the Mountains jersey for a seventh time.

posed humiliation during Festina Affair doping scandal that erupted in the 1998 Tour. "You know all he talks about is attacking. Other riders, they talk about girls, about cars. Virenque, he drives others on the team crazy because all he talks about is attacking, attacking, attacking."

Starting the day over 12 minutes behind race leader Thomas Voeckler, and a solid three minutes behind overall race favorite Lance Arm-

strong, Virenque was in a perfect position since he really didn't threaten either rider.

And just like last year on the first mountain stage into Morzine, the Tour de France race radio announced that Virenque was on the attack early into the stage, too early for any reasonable rider. But then along with subtlety, reason has never been a Virenque strength either.

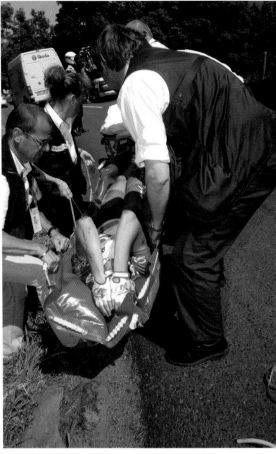

Above: For Sébastian Hinault, the Tour de France ended after a crash on the road to St.-Flour late into stage 10.

Left: Participating in just one of the Tour traditions, Tour riders make morning phone calls from the start village.

"You've got to be a little crazy to attack so early," Virenque would say later, using an adjective that is often applied to him. "Especially since there were 240-kilometres to go. In mo-

With Richard Virenque up the road, Lance Armstrong is content to simply ride in the pack over the Puy Marie climb, in the first mountain stage of this year's Tour.

ments like those, you don't think too much about the finish. You just go."

And off he went.

Along with Belgian cyclist Axel Merckx, who managed to stay with him for over a 150 kilometers, the two charged along up the road and over the day's first climbs. Virenque was clearly trying to score points in the best-climber category, in an effort to become the first rider to win seven polka-dot jersey's awarded each year to the race's best overall climber.

Although no longer able to climb as he did in his prime, Virenque knows he can score significant points in the best-climber category by attacking early, and so he does it often. It's a tactic he has used before. Everyone knew that too, of course. But no one,

save Merckx, seemed able to do anything about it.

And what everyone apparently wanted to forget is that, once Virenque establishes a significant gap, it is very hard, if not impossible, to bring him back. At 34, he may no longer be able to climb with the best, but he is a resilient long-breakaway rider.

And then there are his supporters. He won their hearts when he was in his prime, and they have remained faithful to their idol, even during his worst moments, like when he admitted to doping in the Festina Affair after years of denial and ridicule.

He feeds off his fans. And despite the fact that this was Bastille Day, signs of "Allez Richard," seemed to outnumber the blue, white, and red French flags. And as his lead increased to over 10 minutes, it soon

Facing page: Showing his best condition in years, American Bobby Julich climbs at the front of the pack on stage 10.

Right: He's off and running. Frenchman Richard Virenque in the midst of another one of his memorable breakaways, leading up to his victory in stage 10 to St.-Flour. It would be his last great Tour de France ride.

became clear than neither the yellow jersey, nor any other riders in the peloton would see Virenque before day's end.

Screaming across the line, with his trademark gesture of fingers pointing in the air, Virenque had clearly scored another coup.

"I really asked myself what I was doing midway through the stage. Was I really going to make it? But I just had to keep going."

About winning on Bastille Day, he, like his fans seemed to overlook such details. "No it wasn't premeditated," he said. He was just looking for an occasion to make his mark, a chance to have one more day in the sun.

Above: Under the watchful eye of two of his prize stuffed lions, presented daily to the wearer of the yellow jersey, Frenchman Thomas Voeckler suits up for another day in the yellow jersey. Although jovial, he knows this will be his hardest day yet, as the Tour enters the mountains for the first time on stage 10, with seven climbs scheduled on the roads between Limoges and St.-Flour.

Left: Fulfilling his promise, Frenchman Sandy Casar wears the white jersey on stage 10, as the best young rider in the race.

Stage 11: Ullrich's Secret Weapon

"**Y**OU WANT to know who's really flying right now," asked American cyclist Christian Vandevelde before the start of Tour de France stage 11 in St.-Flour, a small agricultural village tucked away in the heart of France. "Kloeden, Andreas Kloeden. Nobody's talking about him, but he looks really, really strong. He's really cut and riding easily."

Vandevelde, who currently rides for the Spanish Liberty Seguros team, is speaking of the 29-year-old German national champion and teammate to Jan Ullrich, Lance Armstrong's chief rival.

Kloeden is no stranger to the spotlight. When he blasted on the professional cycling scene in 2000, winning the prestigious Paris–Nice in France and Tour of the Basque Country in Spain, many thought Germany had found a new Jan Ullrich. But he failed to confirm the promise. And as year after empty year followed, some thought his moment of glory instead

qualified for Andy Warhol's five minutes of fame.

But he may well be exiting his long tunnel of obscurity, as he has ridden strong, and at times brilliantly in recent months. Just the week before the Tour de France started, Kloeden so-

Laying low before the start of stage 11, German rider Andreas Kloeden, seen here with the jersey distinguishing the German national champion, signed up for this year's Tour as a support rider to his friend and T-Mobile team leader Jan Ullrich. By the end of the Tour, however, he would become the team leader, eventually finishing second to Lance Armstrong.

loed to an impressive win in the German national championships, disposing of proven stars like Erik Zabel and Ullrich himself, with the race's repeated climbs.

And yesterday, on the Tour's first mountain stage in the Massif Central, it was Kloeden who often led the peloton, and who set the tempo on the super steep Puy Mary climb, before eventually finishing second.

Relaxed at the start this morning, Kloeden was visibly pleased to again be riding well. "Yeah I have good condition again. After 2000, I had many problems, first with my knees, then with my back, but I'm riding well now that's true. I hope to be good for Jan. We'll see tomorrow."

Kloeden was speaking of Friday's stage in the Pyrenees that finishes at La Mongie, an eye-sore of a ski resort

Above: Making use of one of the many facilities in the start village, a Tour cyclist gets a haircut before the start of stage 11.

Left: Australian rider Robbie McEwen is ushered toward the podium in the green points jersey.

near the top of the famed Tourmalet Pass that receives momentary respite every time the Tour passes. And ever since 1910, the Tour attacks this climb nearly annually. It was here that Lance Armstrong dropped all his op-

In a timeless scene, the pack races by a country café on stage 11 to the cheers of its onlookers.

ponents just two years ago and captured the yellow jersey on what became his fourth Tour de France victory.

"I think Armstrong's team will go very hard, and we'll have to see," he said. "The last five or six kilometers, it will be up to Jan [Ullrich]."

Of Ullrich's chances against Armstrong, he is confident. "From a sheer power perspective, Jan is super strong. I am confident he is strong enough to win."

So far in this Tour, Ullrich has been virtually invisible, trailing Armstrong by 55 seconds in the overall classification. Kloeden, however, is particularly well-placed to read his leader's legs. As youngsters, the two both attended the German Sports Institute in Berlin, and later both lived and trained together in Merdingen, a town in Germany's Black Forest. When Ullrich decided to move to Switzerland to be closer to the mountains, Kloeden joined him.

"They're real friends," says Philippe Le Gars, who follows Ullrich regularly for the French sports daily *L'Équipe*. "There are not two riders who are better friends, so Ullrich will really be able to count on him when the Tour gets tough."

In fact, some expect Kloeden to take over the responsibilities of Alexander Vinokourov—the T-Mobile rider who forfeited after crashing in the Tour of Switzerland—as a sort of joker to Ullrich and the team, someone who could attack, hence putting

Despite great hopes, Spanish star Iban Mayo rode aimlessly through the race until he finally dropped out in the Pyrenees mountains to the great disappointment of his fans from the Basque country.

Ullrich's adversaries on the defensive, and someone who could also finish high in the overall standings.

"A joker, yes perhaps," he said, apparently favorable to the role, although he shies from comparisons to

Local hero David Moncoutie winning stage 11 after a long solo breakaway in front of his fans in Figeac.

the experienced Vinokourov, who finished third in last year's Tour. "We'll see," he says simply. "We'll see."

Frenchman Didier Rous, a teammate to Thomas Voeckler, discusses the chances of the yellow jersey as the Tour approaches the mountains.

Stage 12: Lance... But of Course

THE TOUR DE FRANCE is nothing if not weeks of speculation. Every day it seems, fans, journalists as well as the Tour cyclists spend much of their free time trading the latest anecdotes concerning the race favorites.

Lance Armstrong, however, put an end to all speculation today, as he devastated nearly all of his challengers and took out a firm lease on the overall victory.

No, Armstrong is not one to beat around the bush. And in vintage fashion, he used the first stage in the mountains, this time in the Pyrenees, to destroy his competition and once again show that why even the French call him "The Boss."

Certain speculators opined that today's stage would not be the crucial stage in the Pyrenees. After all the

Amidst a swarm of fans, Lance Armstrong focuses on the final kilometer of the Tourmalet Pass. Although this is only the Tour's first day in the Pyrenees, already most of his rivals are well behind him.

197.5-kilometer stage was largely flat, finishing with two climbs, the Aspin Pass and the climb to La Mongie—good climbs both of them, but not the best the Pyrenees has to offer the Tour's cyclist.

Little matter, using the Aspin Pass to tire his opponents, he then dusted them. Driving rains that met the pack at the foot of the Aspin climb also favored Armstrong, who thrives under such conditions, while others wilt. With Armstrong's U.S. Postal team commanding the front, Tyler Hamilton first fell off the pace, 7 kilometers

Above and left: American Tyler Hamilton appeared to be all smiles prior to the start of stage 12. Several hours later, however, his spirits would sink as he was dropped on the first climbing day in the Pyrenees due to back problems. His Tour would soon come to a premature end.

Facing page: Jan Ullrich, longtime rival to Lance Armstrong, could only grimace as he watched his Tour de France chances evaporate on the Tourmalet climb. He would finish over two minutes behind Armstrong by the finish.

from the finish. Jan Ullrich was the next casualty less than a kilometer later. Suddenly two of Armstrong's best-placed challengers were riding themselves out of the running in this year's race.

Some, like Ullrich, who would lose two and a half minutes by day's end, would complain about the rains. Others simply complained about their legs and lungs.

Instead, only the promising Ivan Basso who managed to follow Armstrong all the way to the finish and eventually win the stage. Armstrong put up little fight, knowing that he had taken a huge step toward winning a record-setting sixth Tour de France, regardless who won the stage.

Germany's Andreas Kloeden finished just 20 seconds behind. Suddenly the rider who barely 24 hours earlier was no more than a T-Mobile

Above: Diehard Tour fans, showing off 20-year-old Tour hats, take a break from the crowd frenzy after lead riders have passed on the Tourmalet Pass.

Left: Weathering the elements in anticipation, Tour fans greet the pre-race caravan as it climbs the Tourmalet Pass.

Above: Alexander Botcharov, of Russia, pushes toward the finish in La Mongie on the Tourmalet Pass.

Right: In front of his orange-clad fans from the Spanish Basque country, climbing star Iban Mayo offered little to cheer about, as he finished well off the pace on the day that everyone expected him to dominate.

team joker was a potential threat for Tour victory himself.

Thomas Voeckler, the current yellow jersey, could do little in the face of Armstrong, as he too folded early on the final climb. He still rode with plenty of guts, enough to hold onto his jersey for another day. But his 9-minute 35-second lead at the start is now only 5 minutes and 24 seconds. How much longer can he hold on?

Armstrong, who admitted that he was surprised by the non-performances of Ullrich and Hamilton, showed no surprise in Basso's strong performance. Already at the start of the season, the Texan picked Basso to be one of the great Tour revelations this year, after the 26-year-old finished 11th and 7th in the last two Tours.

"He was super strong," Armstrong said of Basso. But according to Basso,

it is Armstrong who is the strongest in the race. Armstrong, he said, remains the man to beat.

Although he lost almost half of his nearly 10-minute lead as he struggled up the Tourmalet Pass at the finish in La Mongie, Thomas Voeckler still managed to save his shirt, keeping the coveted yellow jersey for yet another day.

Stage 13: Courage With a Capital "C"

IT WAS ONE of those days that makes a career. Heck, it was one of those days that make a life. Twenty-four year-old French cyclist Thomas Voeckler has been the surprise of this year's Tour de France.

But no surprise was bigger than today's. In an effort that can only be described as valiant and heroic, Voeckler battled back to hold onto the yellow jersey for at least one more day, a feat few, including he himself, thought plausible.

The day before, Voeckler lost nearly half of his 9-minute 35-second lead on five-time Tour champ Lance Armstrong, when he folded on the stage to the Pyrenees ski-resort of La Mongie. The stage on this day, number 13 in this year's Tour de France, promised to be even tougher as the peloton tackled no less than seven climbs before finishing on the

In the advertising caravan that precedes the riders, even Mickey Mouse has been known to ride in the Tour.

leg-breaking and endless Plateau de Beille climb.

Right from the start, pre-race favorites like Haimar Zubeldia, Tyler Hamilton, and Denis Menchov all showed signs of wear and tear. All eventually dropped out. Iban Mayo fared little better, dropping on the third climb of the day, he finally finished 40 minutes behind. Voeckler, never one to make cycling look easy, did as he had done all week: He just kept plugging along.

Finally though, he cracked on the fourth climb of the day, the Agnes Pass. With two climbs, not to mention nearly 60 kilometres remaining, many figured that the Frenchman had finally lost his yellow shirt. Sure, the famed golden fleece is know to transform riders, pushing them to ride be-

yond their normal level. But even such transformations have their limits. Voeckler seemed to hit his.

But no! The Brioches le Boulangère rider showed that he had at least one more fight in him before he would surrender his jersey to Lance Armstrong, its likely heir. He had a final word to say before returning to the faceless ranks of the peloton.

Battling back on the descent, he again caught the Armstrong group and held with them until the foot of the final Plateau de Beille climb, a menacing 17-kilometer wall. And although he was soon dropped on the steep early sections of the climb, he never unraveled. He simply rode at his own pace and even caught riders dropped after him. By the finish, he held a grip, albeit a small one, on the

Facing page: For the second day in a row, only Italian Ivan Basso could follow Lance Armstrong as the American destroyed the competition in the Pyrenees. Here he leads Basso up the Plateau de Beille.

Right: Spiderman takes on the Tour de France, advertizing his new movie in the publicity caravan.

race lead, with 22 seconds still separating him from Armstrong.

"All day long, I heard, 'yellow jersey dropped, yellow jersey dropped,' then 'yellow jersey returns, yellow jersey returns'," said Armstrong, the day's eventual winner, who is now in second place overall and in a com-

manding position to win a record-breaking sixth Tour title. "He absolutely deserves to keep it [the jersey]. I'm very, very, very impressed."

"I suffered all day long," said a visibly relieved Voeckler. "Yesterday, I was disappointed to lose so much time. When I climbed on the podium

yesterday, I thought it was my last day. Not many people were betting on me, and I was the first. I'm surprised to still be in yellow. I impressed myself."

Needless to say, he impressed many more people than himself. And no one will be surprised when Thomas Voeckler produces another exploit.

Above: Thomas Voeckler managed to hang on to his yellow jersey longer than anyone had expected.

Left: Dutch rider Michael Boogerd gets some encouragement from orange-clad Basque fans as he rides toward the Plateau de Beille finish on stage 13.

Stage 14: Who is Ivan Basso?

IN THIS TOUR DE FRANCE of surprises, few are bigger than that of Italy's Ivan Basso. Some of course predicted that this year's race would again be a two-up *mano-a-mano*.

The only rider to rival Lance Armstrong in the Pyrenees, Italian Ivan Basso suddenly became the revelation of the Tour.

But few would have predicted that Lance Armstrong's main challenge would come, not from Germany's Jan Ullrich, but rather from the 26-year-old Basso.

One person who is not surprised, however, is Armstrong. Already at the beginning of the season, the five-time Tour winner predicted that Basso would be one of the great revelations of this year's race.

But with the total collapse of more proven challengers like Spain's Iban Mayo and American Tyler Hamilton, it is Basso who now remains Armstrong's only apparent menace. He was the only rider capable of following Armstrong in the Pyrenees, dropping all others on both mountains stages. On the stage to La Mongie, Basso claimed the victory, while on the Plateau de Beille it was Armstrong who took the stage honors, with Basso on his wheel.

And now, as the race heads toward the Alps in the final week of racing, Basso is only 1 minute 17 seconds down on the Texan. Frenchman

Thomas Voeckler, who has the yellow jersey by 22 seconds over Armstrong, is not expected to hold the lead once the race hits the Alpes.

Basso, however, promises to stick close to the American all the way to Paris, and it is still not known just how much of a challenge he can really maintain. After finishing 11th in the 2002 Tour as the best young rider,

and 7th last year, Basso is clearly still maturing. But how much has he improved on year's past?

"That's one guy who just dreams about the Tour de France," says American Bobby Julich, who rides with Basso on the Danish CSC team this year. Julich rode strongly on the

Above: Fans line the streets of Nimes just for a glimpse of the Tour.

Left: Dressed in their own yellow jerseys, children in the southwestern town of Carcassone wait patiently before the start of stage 14 for a Tour cyclist to stop and add to their autograph collections.

Facing page: Always focused, Armstrong prepares for stage 14, a comparatively quiet stage between the Pyrenees and the Alps.

first stage in the Pyrenees, before crashing on the stage to Plateau de Beille. Denying obvious pain—not to mention an injury that would eventually be diagnosed as a fractured wrist—he still suited up for the start, ready to pedal on. At the start of stage 14 in Carcassonne, a town that prides itself on its famous *cassoulet*, white

bean-and-sausage stew, when it's not welcoming the Tour to town. "If it wasn't for Ivan, I'd be out of here,"

Julich said, still in obvious pain. Looking over toward the CSC team bus where Basso posed with his wife and

Getting a look at the yellow jersey as the Tour passes through town can be a fleeting affair.

The peloton races through the streets of Nimes on its way to the stage 14 finish.

baby for a photo op, Julich could only hope for better days to come. "But

with Ivan up there, I've got something to ride for. It gives me an objective."

According to his CSC team director Bjarne Riis, winner of the 1996 Tour, Basso is one of the great riders of the future. "He's a tremendous climber, but his greatest quality for me is simply his ability to recover, day in and day out. For a race like the Tour de France, that is essential."

So far in the mountains it is impossible to tell who is stronger—Armstrong or Basso. After all, neither has yet made a full all-out attack, as the two simply rode away from all other riders on both stages in the Pyrenees. But the big question mark remains time trialing, previously a weakness for Basso.

Under the guidance of Riis, Basso has focused on this weakness since leaving the Italian Fassa Bortolo team to ride for CSC this year. "Before ,with Fassa, we just worked on time trialing a week or so before the Tour, but with Bjarne we've been working on it all year." Among other aspects of specific training, Basso went to Boston this winter for special wind-tunnel testing.

And if the Italian national time trial championships are any gauge—and they may or may not be—Basso finished fourth, only 20 seconds behind little-known winner Dario Cioni. For Basso, the effort was clearly more of a training ride. "I think I could have actually won it," he said. "But I did three long training rides the three days before the event."

Of the Alpe d'Huez time trial, Basso is confident he can ride with the best. The final 60-kilometer time trial in Besançon appears more dubious. "Normally, I will lose two to three minutes on the top guys."

But Basso is clearly a new rider. Always amiable, he is not one to make bold predictions. Armstrong, he says, "is unbeatable." But at the same time, he is not yet ready to say that he is riding for second place.

After all, the Tour still has a week to go.

Spaniard Aitor Gonzalez races toward the stage 14 victory in Nimes.

Stage 15: Who's Leading T-Mobile?

GERMANS, IT IS SAID, like to keeps things "*in Ordnung*," in order. If so, then there must be a lot of unease within the T-Mobile cycling team these days. Ever since their team leader Jan Ullrich folded in the Pyrenees, only to be effaced by the sudden rise of his long-time teammate Andreas Kloeden, there has been an uncharacteristic lack of direction within what is known as one of the most organized cycling teams in the world.

While Kloeden is now in third place, three minutes 22 seconds behind Lance Armstrong, who recaptured the yellow jersey today after winning stage 15, Ullrich moved to fifth place, 6 minutes 54 seconds back. The performances of the two beg the question, "who is leading this team?"

The team's manager, Walter Godefroot, admits, "I don't know yet."

Trouble started when Ullrich cracked on the first climbing stage in the Pyrenees, early on the final climb to La Mongie. Suddenly, the plot line for the German team was thrown into disarray. For a team not known for its ability to ad lib, such a scenario promised to be troublesome.

When Kloeden asked his team director, Mario Kummer, what to do, he was told to continue at his own pace. Ullrich's personal trainer Rudy Pevenage was outraged, however, stating simply, "do you think Armstrong's teammate would just ride on if he was in trouble?"

After attacking late into stage 15, Jan Ullrich is disappointed to once again lose to Lance Armstrong.

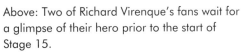

Above: Two of Richard Virenque's fans wait for a glimpse of their hero prior to the start of Stage 15.

Left: Thomas Voeckler, moments after crossing the finish line on stage 15 and losing the yellow jersey.

Kummer seems to feel that Kloeden is the team's real joker this year, and wasn't willing to waste him on a floundering Ullrich. Godefroot, however, hesitates, saying that "while Kloeden is in the best shape of his life, he is still no Jan Ullrich."

Confusing? Yes, anything but "*in Ordnung.*"

Nobody within the team seems to understand why Ullrich rode so poorly in the Pyrenees as he appears more fit and trim than ever before. But the T-Mobile staff cannot decide on just how good Kloeden can be. Af-

ter all only weeks before the 2004 started Kloeden was clearly consid- ered a teammate, nothing more, nothing less.

To get a good vantage point on the day the Tour passes, fans camp out for days in advance along the road leading up to the Alpe d'Huez.

Facing page: The *grupetto*, or group of stragglers, make their way to the finish on stage 15 in Villard de Lans.

Below: Ivan Basso talks with the press after narrowly losing stage 15 to Lance Armstrong.

But that was before Alexander Vinokourov crashed in the Tour of Switzerland and had to forfeit his Tour

and other riders like Paolo Salvodelli or Cadel Evans, all expected to play a role in the T-Mobile Tour team, failed to even make the team.

For the moment, it seems both Kloeden and Ullrich are the team's protected riders. But such status, we have seen, can be ephemeral come Tour time.

Kloeden says, " I will still work for Jan if necessary." Never one to deviate, Ullrich also says, "I will work for Andreas if necessary." Whom to believe? Apparently, the race will decide.

Today, on the stage from Valreas to Villard de Lans, a 180-kilometer jaunt from French Provence through the foothills of the Alpes, Ullrich tried to salvage his disastrous Tour by at-

tacking some 60 kilometers from the finish. It was a good move, as he initially gained over a minute on Armstrong. Kloeden simply sat patiently on the American's wheel. Eventually though, Ullrich was caught. And then in the final, Kloeden gave Ullrich a lead-out in an attempt to help him win the stage. That move also failed, as he could do no better than third behind a victorious Armstrong.

We'll have a better idea after the time trial tomorrow," said Godefroot, speaking of the much-anticipated time trial up the mythic Alpe d'Huez mountain on Wednesday. "We'll decide then."

Maybe they will, but then again, maybe they won't. If either rider folds, the decision will be easy. However, if Kloeden and Ullrich remain close after Alpe d'Huez, then the search for T-Mobile's "*Ordnung*," could well continue.

Lance Armstrong receives a kiss from his girlfriend, Sheryl Crow, after taking over the yellow jersey on stage 15.

Stage 16: Who'll Get Podium Honors?

AFTER SLAUGHTERING his competition on the much anticipated Alpe d'Huez time trial, Lance Armstrong now appears certain to win a record-setting sixth Tour de France.

But in his wake, a real battle for the other two places on the final victory podium is shaping up between Italy's Ivan Basso and Germany's Andreas Kloden and Jan Ullrich.

Basso, until now an equal to Armstrong in the mountains, floundered terribly in today's race against the clock, losing two minutes 23 seconds to the American, one minute 22 seconds to Ullrich, and 37 seconds to Kloeden. As a result, his overall lead

on the two riders with the T-Mobile team has weakened, as he now holds a one minute 15-second lead on

Ivan Basso cracked on the Alpe d'Huez time trial, losing a horrendous 2 minutes 23 seconds in only 15.5 kilometers to Lance Armstrong. Suddenly, even his chance to finish second in the Tour was in jeopardy.

Kloeden overall and a four minute seven second lead on Ullrich.

For many, such time gaps would suffice; but Basso is vulnerable in the time trialing, and the final 60-kilometer race against the clock in Besançon on Saturday could prove to be his undoing. Today, as a climber, he hoped to hold his own. Instead, he lost significant time to Ullrich over only 15.5 kilometers. What can the German do to

him on a significantly flatter 60 kilometers? And with barely a minute on Kloeden, also a strong time trialer, Basso could realistically lose the podium on the final time trial, unless of course he gains more time on tomorrow's mountains stage from Bourg d'Oisans to Le Grand Bornand.

Interestingly, however, it is T-Mobile who appears to be in the attacking mood, not Basso's CSC team.

Bjarne Riis, Basso's director, still does not understand what went wrong on the Alpe d'Huez today. But he doesn't appear ready to make any moves to gain more time in the mountains. "I didn't really expect him [Ivan] to lose so much time, but I

Above: Visibly exhausted after the Alpe d'Huez time trial, Austrian cyclist George Totschnig was nevertheless content to be in seventh place overall, his best Tour performance to date.

Left: As in each of Lance Armstrong's first five Tour victories, fellow American George Hincapie again proved invaluable.

could tell from the beginning that he didn't have rhythm. Lance [Armstrong] was fantastic, and he definitely won the Tour today. Now it is up to T-Mobile to attack. We'll see tomorrow who is more dangerous, Kloeden or Ullrich."

Riis said he expected tomorrow's stage to be much like the Plateau de Beille stage in the Pyrenees, with the U.S. Postal team riding strong tempo

Above: American Levi Leipheimer, seen here on the Alpe d'Huez, would finish in the top ten of the Tour for a second time in three years.

Left: Lance Armstrong, moments after winning the stage 16 time trial on Alpe d'Huez.

and forcing a grueling race of attrition.

After his strong time trial today, Kloeden confirmed that T-Mobile planned to race aggressively in an effort to have both of their riders finish on the podium. "Tomorrow we will try to attack. It is the last difficult mountain stage so we have to."

Riis seems content to ride defensively. And he also has confidence that Basso will bounce back. "I think Ivan cracked under pressure, but I am confident he will be as strong tomorrow as in all other mountain stages. I'm confident Ivan will be on the podium."

Above: American Floyd Landis proved to be one of Lance Armstrong's most valuable teammates in this year's Tour.

American Bobby Julich gets his jersey ready prior to the start of stage 17.

Stage 17: The End for Armstrong?

AFTER WINNING his third-straight stage in this year's Tour de France today, Lance Armstrong is cruising to a record-setting sixth Tour victory. But while this year's Tour may well be his easiest victory, it may also be his last.

Asked at the start of stage 17 in the mountain town of Bourg d'Oisans about the possibility of Armstrong

According *Bicycling* magazine's Tour de France site, Armstrong might not compete in the 2005 Tour. A senior official with the Amaury Sports Organization, speaking on condition of anonymity, said that his conversations with Postal officials led him to believe Armstrong would not return to the Tour next year, but would branch out to other races such as the Giro d'Italia and Vuelta España, or one-day classics like Liège–Bastogne–Liège or the Amstel Gold Race.

After finishing the Alpe d'Huez time trial, Frenchman Richard Virenque has a virtual lock on the polka-dot jersey awarded to best climber for a record-setting seventh year.

missing next year's Tour, Postal officials would not admit to any plans. "We didn't talk about the program of next year yet," said Postal's team director Johan Bruyneel. "I don't know, a lot of things can change, a lot of things can happen."

Already this past June, hints that Armstrong may not ride the 2005 Tour arose when the American flew to Silver Spring, Maryland, for a sur-prise press conference, the subject of which, as most suspected, was the an-nouncement of a new team sponsor.

At the hastily arranged press conference, Armstrong stood alongside executives of Discovery Communications, a major owner of cable television networks, as they announced a "multi-year, multi-million dollar com-mitment" to Armstrong's team.

As Armstrong stood by, Discovery Networks' President Billy Campbell held up a simple black-and-white jersey with a Discovery logo and said, "We wanted to show everyone how great you will look when you clinch your seventh win in 2005."

Above: After losing the yellow jersey on stage 15, Thomas Voeckler now tries to defend the white jersey awarded to the best young rider. It will prove to be yet another losing battle.

Left: A rather excited fan takes a cigarette break while cheering on a Tour cyclist on stage 17.

Amid applause, Armstrong simply crossed his fingers and replied, "Let's get through number six first, shall we?"

When asked about the team's Tour plans in 2005 now that Armstrong has cinched a record-breaking sixth Tour title, Bruyneel was non-committal. "He [Lance] is going to race [in 2005], but we didn't decide a program," said Bruyneel. "Now with the UCI Pro Tour, the whole team program changes. In my opinion, riding the Giro and the Vuelta is not the same, but we'll see."

The Pro Tour, the UCI's most significant overhaul of the structure of professional cycling since reverting to trade team affiliations in the post-war Tour era, is a series of 25–30 races that must be contested by each of the Pro Tour teams. As a Pro Tour team, Discovery would have to send a team to each race.

Armstrong, the ASO official said, wants to support the Pro Tour by lending his presence to races other than the Tour de France.

Bill Stapleton, founder of Capital Sports and Entertainment, Armstrong's agent, and CEO of Tailwind Sports, which owns the team, said it's far too early to say whether Armstrong would not race the Tour again.

"We haven't even discussed that yet," he said when asked about it this morning. "No decisions have been made. It would definitely be incorrect to say we won't be back."

When asked if he planned to ride the 2005 Tour, Armstrong told *Bicycling* he had no comment.

Such a decision would not be without precedence. Jacques Anquetil, the race's first five-time win-

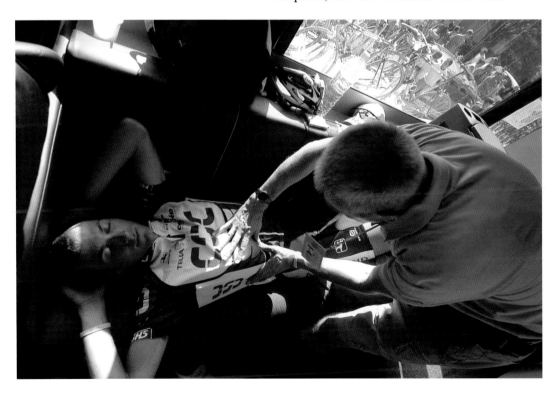

Ivan Basso working through breathing exercises prior to the start of stage 17 in Bourg d'Oisans.

ner, simply opted not to race in 1965 after winning his fifth in 1964. "What good would it do me to win yet another Tour," Anquetil said at the time. Instead, he set new objectives, like winning the ultra-marathon Bordeaux–Paris race only hours after winning the Dauphiné-Liberé race.

But does Armstrong really have enough interest in races other than the Tour, an event he has virtually given his lifc to? In addition, the Tour has grown to disproportionate proportions of prestige and popularity.

The ASO source conceded that it might be outside Armstrong's nature to leave the Tour de France—if a sixth Tour, why not a seventh? But he added that Armstrong has immense respect for other members of the five-time winners club and does not want to go overboard in setting a new record. Besides, he wants to open up the Tour de France to new faces and challengers.

Perhaps the best indications of Armstrong's thoughts on a possible seventh Tour come from the man himself. At the Discovery press conference, he said he would definitely race at least in 2005 but stopped short of committing to the Tour.

"You're a smart man," he laughed when asked if he ever thought of changing his race priorities. "I do want to do that. I'm torn because the Tour is so big and it is truly the event that means the most to cycling and to me. But there are days when I think about the classics in the springtime in Belgium; I think about the World Championships; I think about the Hour Record; I think about the Giro or the Vuelta and I really want to—

Left: A morning ritual, the CSC team participates in their daily pre-stage meeting.

Facing page: Lance Armstrong leads the charge over the final climb, the Croix Fry Pass on stage 17. He went on to win his third consecutive stage in the race.

not necessarily win those events—but I want to do them. The Giro I've never even done. So to do 12 or 13 or 14 years professionally, and have to say you never did the Giro, I think would be a shame."

Discovery officials also said at the press conference that they supported Armstrong's eventual wishes to

branch out more, whether in the sport or outside of it. "One thing we did do is say to him and his team," said Campbell at the press conference, "that they can focus, as long as they want, on continuing to win the Tours, but the minute he wants to take a little break or have some other side interest, we're there."

At the U.S. press conference, Armstrong reflected on his future. "I guess, thinking out loud, you know, maybe do another Tour next year and perhaps in 2006, then focus on some spring classics or something different, but that's a long way off and again, now I need to focus on what I know is going to happen in three week's time and that's the Tour."

On the podium after today's stage win in le Grand Bornand, Armstrong shook hands with five-time winner Bernard Hinault, who told him approvingly, "No gifts," referring to his chasing down Andreas Kloden for the stage. Can an American who's always done everything to the extreme pull back now? Could he really give other riders the gift of a Tour de France title if he still had the legs to win it himself?

Spaniard Carlos Sastre gets a little unexpected help on stage 17.

Stage 18: Yellow Jersey Detour

JUST WHEN Lance Armstrong seemed to be rolling to a trouble-free victory in the Tour de France, he created some trouble for himself. Stage 18 of this year's race, a 166.5-kilometer jaunt from Annemasse to Lons-le-Saunier, was supposed to be one of the quieter days in this year's race.

But in a strange tale of inter-peloton politics, Armstrong made a tactical move that incited talk of doping issues, the last thing he would seemingly need during his moment of glory.

For months now, Armstrong has been feuding with little-known Italian cyclist Filippo Simeoni. The trouble started in 2001 in light of the highly publicized investigation into the working methods of Doctor Michele Ferrari, an Italian doctor charged with administering performance-enhancing drugs to professional cyclists. Simeoni, one of many riders implicated in the

Italian cyclist Filippo Simeoni reflects while telling the press how he was chased down by Lance Armstrong early into stage 18. Between the two riders, no love is lost.

investigation admitted taking the performance-enhancing drug EPO. In his official court testimony, later published in the press, Simeoni stated that Ferrari prescribed him the drug before certain races and gave him directions for taking the drug.

While Simeoni never mentioned Armstrong in his testimony, it has nevertheless compromised the American, since he has admitted that he has had a close working relationship with Ferrari, while Simeoni's testimony provided a clear link between Ferrari and doping.

The matter was complicated when Armstrong publicly called Simeoni a liar on several occasions earlier in 2004, to which the Italian finally responded by suing Armstrong for defamation.

Returning to the stage at hand, the official Tour race radio then lit up when it was announced that the yellow jersey, hence Armstrong, was chasing Simeoni, who was bridging up to an unthreatening early breakaway at the start of the stage.

For Armstrong, the break contained no direct rival. It was clear that his move was simply a symbolic statement directed at Simeoni.

And it was also clear that the move would focus attention on his dual with the Italian, as well as the American's relationship with Ferrari. There would be questions at the finish.

"I was protecting the interests of the peloton," said the soon-to-be six-time Tour-winner after the finish. "He [Simeoni] is not a rider that the peloton likes to be up front, because all he does is attack the peloton and

Selected randomly, German rider Rolf Aldag waits his turn at the Tour drug testing center, a small van parked just after the finish of each stage.

then say bad things about other riders and the group in general."

On reaching the six-rider move, Simeoni said Armstrong looked over at him and smirked, "Bravo. Nice move." When José Vicente Garcia Acosta pleaded with Armstrong to drop back and let the break have an honest chance to continue, Armstrong reportedly told them he would gladly do that, under one condition: Simeoni was not to continue in the break, either. Faced with the choice of sinking the chances of six riders or his own, Simeoni drifted back to the pack, accompanied by Armstrong.

In between, the two riders talked, with Armstrong even briefly placing his hand on Simeoni's shoulder. "Armstrong and I spoke as the peloton was catching us, but I prefer not to say what he said," Simeoni recounted. "It was too serious."

Armstrong's move at best was unnecessary. And it was most certainly controversial. Clearly, Armstrong was exercising his indisputable power as the "*patron*," or boss of the peloton. But what does it mean to be a *patron* of the Tour de France?

Is a *patron* simply the strongest rider of his era, or is there something more? In the true sense of the word, there is: a *patron* is not just a champion, but a godfather of sorts, a man who can dictate the moods and mores of the peloton. Typically, it is also a benefactor of sorts, a man whose magnanimity can elevate the dignity of the sport through observation of its most time-honored precepts, key among them sportsmanship.

On stage 18 we saw a Tour *patron* in action, but it was not a benevolent one.

Despite the rains, French sprinter Jean-Patrick Nazon suits up and prepares for stage 18. Already he is thinking of the final stage into Paris, one he hopes to win like he did the year before.

Simeoni is one of cycling's most anonymous riders. In an 11-year career, he has had just one significant win, a stage of the 2001 Tour of Spain, and as a career gregario, or helper, he has done little to distinguish himself—good or bad. But two years ago Simeoni hurled himself into a most unwelcome and glaring spotlight

when he became a key witness in the ongoing trial of Doctor Michele Ferrari, who was being tried in the

Above: Norwegian cyclist Thor Hushovd, winner of a stage and the yellow jersey earlier in the race, suits up for stage 18, where he hopes to pick up points and recapture the green points jersey.

Right: Fans applaud the winners during the podium ceremony of stage 18.

Facing page: Paris is near, but riders keep attacking. Fans line the roads to cheer an early breakaway over the Col de Faucille on stage 18

Italian province of Bologna for sporting fraud.

In his testimony before the Bologna court on February 12, 2002, Simeoni described how Ferrari showed him how to use the banned red blood cell booster EPO more effectively. Ferrari denied the charges, but Armstrong, in a carefully prepared interview broadcast on RAI TV in Italy on the eve of that year's Milan–San

Remo World Cup opener, said that Simeoni had lied. He repeated the claim in an article in *Le Monde* in April 2003, saying that Simeoni was "a compulsive liar" and had doped long before meeting Ferrari.

In response, Simeoni decided to sue Armstrong for defamation, saying Armstrong's comments had hurt his career. In a lengthy interview published in the French sports daily

L'Équipe during the first week of this year's Tour de France, Simeoni said he had been unfairly singled out by Armstrong. "[Lance] has tried to defend his own image vis-a-vis Ferrari, but I've never accused Armstrong personally. I would never do that," he said to the paper. The lawsuit, he said, was "not a question of money. If I'm awarded money, I'll give it to charity."

With sweat still dripping from his forehead after finally finishing stage 18, Simeoni reflected and said simply, "Armstrong showed by his disappointing action what type of person he was. A real great champion doesn't stoop to such things."

Armstrong said today that he chased down Simeoni "to protect the interests of the peloton." But clearly, he had intentions of his own as well.

Spaniard Juan-Miguel Mercado lunges toward the finish line on his way to winning stage 18.

Stage 19: Hungry for Green

ROBBIE MCEWEN. You may know him as the stout speedster who magically jumped out of the pack to grab stages 2 and 9. Or the Aussie who consistently charges the line—head down—like a mad bull. Going Mach 1 in the last meters is this man's forte—his blessed mission.

American Levi Leipheimer rode consistently throughout this year's Tour to finish an impressive ninth.

Now after lugging up and down tortuous mountain roads in the Pyrenees and the Alps—including a deathly push against time up the Alpe d'Huez—McEwen can hone in on his target: the green sprinters jersey. It's the most sought-after shirt after its more famous cousin the yellow jersey, and for the past two years the winner has been decided in last seconds on the last day over the historic roads of the Champs-Élysées in Paris.

In 2002, McEwen and fellow countryman Stuart O'Grady went head-to-head for the green jersey. McEwen won. Last year McEwen found himself in the race head-to-head with yet another Aussie mate, Baden Cooke. Cooke scooped the green jersey from McEwen in a nerve-wracking, elbow-bumping finish, winning by two points.

This year, the green jersey again comes down to the final stretch, and again McEwen is leading the contin-

gent. Thor Hushovd, stage 8 winner and yellow jersey wearer for one day, is on his wheel this year, trailing by 12 points in the green classification. The race isn't as tight as it was in previous years, but it's not in the bag either.

"Mathematically it is possible," said Roger Legeay, director to Hushovd on the Credit Agricole team. "But out on the roads, they [McEwen and Hushovd] are very close."

Above: With a strong performance in the final time trial, Andreas Kloeden moved into second place overall behind Lance Armstrong.

Right: Looking good but struggling, Italian Ivan Basso would slip to third place overall after the Tour's final time trial in Besançon.

Facing page: A lone cyclists pedals on during the Tour's final time trial. For him, as for all other riders in the race, the finish is now only a day away.

In the final stage into Paris, there will be two intermediate sprints with the first, second, and third place riders winning six, points, and two points respectively. And then on the Champs-Élysées the first six riders will earn 35, 30, 26, 24, 22, and 20 points respectively.

"Anything is possible, but it's going to be hard," Hushovd said this morning. "I mean even if I beat him [McEwen] in every sprint, if he is second, he will win."

McEwen is ready for the final stage grudge match. "The last three years it's always the same thing, with lots of pressure. I'm getting used to it. "It's a clean slate," he said. "But I have a 10-point lead."

Though McEwen is quick to point out that the fight for bragging rights on Sunday is not restricted to those in the hunt for the green jersey.

"There are a lot of guys who suffered through the mountains just to have a chance here. There are a lot of guys that are hungry."

Putting the final touches on a technically flawless Tour de France, Lance Armstrong powers to yet another stage victory in the final time trial to win the race for an unprecedented sixth time.

Stage 20: Armstrong Alone at the Summit

THE SUN is setting on the Champs-Élysées, and Lance Armstrong has made cycling history. As he takes his final victory lap with his U.S. Postal teammates, the American can soak up the cheers of the thousands of fans and bask in his own satisfaction for a moment, as he has just accomplished something no-one else has ever done before: win six Tours de France, the world's greatest bicycle race.

To go where no man has gone before, that is what Lance Armstrong has just done. Four riders before him, Frenchmen Jacques Anquetil and Bernard Hinault, Belgian Eddy Merckx, and Spain's Miguel Indurain all won five Tours. None did six.

"Maybe tomorrow would be my best day in this year's Tour," Armstrong said last night in his final Tour press conference. "If I make it tomorrow and climb the steps of the podium of the Champs-Élysées, that will be the moment I carry with me forever."

He did, and he will.

Armstrong's quest for history started in Liège, Belgium, at the Tour start three weeks ago. At the time, it appeared that this year's race would be his most difficult as a new host of rivals were eager to challenge the five-time winner.

In a now familiar pose, Lance Armstrong loops around in front of the Arc de Triomphe in Paris, this time on his way to winning his sixth Tour de France—a first in the history of the sport.

"A lot of guys are licking their lips," said fellow American Tyler Hamilton, a friend and rival, at the start. However, from the start in Belgium to the final meters in Paris, Armstrong rode a flawless race, as his rivals cracked and folded.

It can be said that this year's race was made dull by Armstrong's domination. But that was not his fault. It is more the fault of challengers like Spain's Iban Mayo, Germany's Jan Ullrich, as well as Hamilton, all of whom simply failed to produce. Mayo peaked too early this season. Hamilton injured his back in a crash on stage six, and Ullrich simply was ill-prepared.

As a result, Armstrong rarely had to attack in this year's race, something

Above: Danish fans on the Champs Élysées await the Tour.

Right: Although the Tour riders are still in the outskirts of Paris, a group of American fans lead the cheer for Armstrong on the Champs Élysées.

he has done dramatically in the past. Instead, he simply rode away from his opponents to win a total of five stages.

Of all his Tour victories this one is surely the most perfect.

In front of the watchful eye of the Tour's big screen, the pack powers down the Champs Élysées.

So tonight the superlatives abound.

He also has his detractors. At the start in Liège, he was booed and hissed significantly, and he was visibly harassed on mountain stages like the Plateau de Beille and the Alpe d'Huez. Fans who disapprove of the American do so seemingly for several reasons. Some suspect him of the dope allegations that have followed him since winning his first Tour back in 1999. Others seem to resent his take-no-prisoners approach toward racing.

Armstrong takes from all of the previous five-time winners. While his idol was once Miguel Indurain, he has dominated the Tour more like Eddy Merckx, destroying, even humiliating

Above: Armstrong powers down the Champs-Élysées on the final stretch of the 2004 Tour de France.

Left: After winning a historic sixth Tour de France, Lance Armstrong starts his victory lap down the Champs-Élysées.

Facing page: Belgian Tom Boonen wins his second stage of the Tour on the Champs-Élysées.

his competition both in the mountains and the time trials. But in his personality can be found a bit of both Jacques Anquetil and Bernard Hinault. Like Anquetil, he has a cool edge about him, while like Hinault, he can sometimes be wildly aggressive, even hostile. And like both of them, he had no problem putting winning before everything else.

"If Jacques Anquetil was here, he would say that they [the public] booed him all day, and Eddy Merckx told me they booed him too," Armstrong said. "It's comforting for me to know that some of the greatest champions were booed. So I'm in good company. Sometimes in France they prefer the guy who gets second. But if that's the choice—to be loved or to win, I'll take winning."

Clearly, Armstrong has made his choice. And it has served him well.

On the final victory podium of the 2004 Tour de France. From left to right: Robbie McEwen, winner of the points jersey; Lance Armstrong, winner of the yellow jersey; Richard Virenque, winner of the polka-dot jersey for the best climber; and Wladimir Karpets, winner of the white jersey for the best young rider.